What's
Kay Cook'N

VOL 1
SIMPLE
HOME COOKING
KAY MASON

ISBN: 978-0-578-73512-2
Library of Congress: 2020913965
Edited by: Keyoka Kinzy
Cover: Write on Promotions
Layout: Write On Promotions

Dedication

I dedicate this book to my #1, my beautiful daughter, Chelcè, who stayed on me to get this book completed. She gave me words of encouragement and cheered me on to the completion. Thank you for being my bright light every day and loving me through everything. I love you to infinity!

To my beautiful, courageous, and hard-working mother, I thank you for all the unconditional love you have given me. I will never forget how you supported me and encouraged my creativity. I want to thank you for coming home after long hard day of work to cook a hot meal for us. I know that being a single parent, who worked two jobs, was incredibly challenging for you, but you never complained about it. Thank you and I love you, Mom.

Acknowledgements and Thanks

I want to send a special thank you to Karl, my brother, for all the food challenges we did as teens. The food challenges with him started my love for cooking.

Thank you to my grandmothers, for all of the recipes that I will continue to use and pass down. Thanks for showing me how to bake and allowing me to destroy your kitchen. I want to also thank my grandfather, for inspiring me to start a garden.

Lastly, my friends, thank you for encouraging me to follow my dreams and for being my tasters

Love Always,

Kay

CONTENTS

CONTENTS

WHATS KAY
COOK'N

Chapter 1

SALADS

Asian Salad with Ginger Glazed

Serves 4 // Time: 30 minutes

Ingredients for Salad

3 boneless, skinless chicken breast or thighs

2 romaine lettuces, chopped

2 cups Napa cabbage, shredded

1 cup red cabbage, shredded

1 ½ cup carrots, grated

4 green onions, thinly sliced

½ cup cilantro, chopped

¼ cup cashews, chopped (optional)

¼ cup fried wonton chips

Ingredients for Marinade

2 tablespoon soy sauce

1 teaspoon garlic powder

½ teaspoon five spice powder

1 teaspoon sesame oil

½ teaspoon pepper

½ teaspoon red pepper flakes

1 garlic clove, minced

1 tablespoon ginger, minced
Olive oil for sauté

Ingredients for Salad Dressing

¼ cup rice vinegar

1 tablespoon sesame oil

1 tablespoon reduced sodium soy sauce

1 tablespoon brown sugar

1 garlic clove, minced

1 teaspoon ginger, minced

1 teaspoon hoisin sauce

Ingredients for Glaze

2 tablespoon minced ginger

2 tablespoon sesame seeds

2 tablespoon sesame oil

2 tablespoon brown sugar

2 tablespoon of the soy sauce

1 teaspoon black pepper

Preparation:

1. In a large bowl, combine the ingredients for the marinade. In a gallon-sized Ziploc bag or large bowl, add chicken and marinade. Marinate for at least 1 hour. Drain the chicken from the marinade.

2. Salad dressing: In a small bowl, whisk together all of the ingredients to combine. Set aside.

3. Glaze: In a small bowl, whisk together all of the ingredients to combine. Remove chicken from marinade bag and pat dry with a paper towel.

In large skillet, heat on medium heat, add olive oil to coat the bottom of the skillet, and add chicken. Cook chicken, turning occasionally and brushing chicken with glaze, until done. (Chicken is done when the internal temperature reaches 165 degrees F. Anything higher will overcook and dry out the chicken). Let chicken cool, then chop into smaller pieces.

4. In a large serving bowl, combine romaine lettuce and Napa cabbage. Top with chicken, red cabbage, carrots, cilantro, cashews, and green onions. Pour the salad dressing over the salad and gently toss to combine. Top with fried wonton chips.

5. Serve immediately.

Broccoli Pasta Salad

Serves 6-8 // Time: 1 hour 15 minutes

Ingredients for Salad

1 ½ cup shell or bow tie pasta, cooked

3 broccoli crowns, chopped

2 cups green or red, seedless grapes, quartered

6 pieces of thick bacon, cooked and chopped (optional for vegan)

1 cup candied (or plain) walnuts, chopped

⅓ cup green onions, thinly sliced

⅓ cup Splenda or sugar

1 cup mayonnaise (sub with vegan mayonnaise)

½ cup raisins

1 teaspoon salt

⅓ cup red wine vinegar

½ teaspoon crushed red pepper

Preparation:

1. Cut broccoli florets from stems, and separate florets into small pieces. Cut away long stems and chop. Put in a large bowl to set aside.

2. In a small bowl, whisk together mayonnaise, sugar, vinegar, salt, and red pepper until combined and smooth.

3. In a large bowl, add broccoli, grapes, green onions, raisin, bacon, and pasta. Pour in mayonnaise mixture and toss to combine. Cover and put in the refrigerator for at least 3 hours or overnight.

4. When ready to eat, sprinkle in walnuts, toss, and serve.

Kale Salad with Candied Walnuts and Apples

Serves 6 // Time: 30 minutes

Ingredients for Salad

½ cup olive oil

¼ cup fresh lemon juice

2 tablespoon honey

1 teaspoon garlic, minced

1 small red onion, thinly sliced

1 ½ teaspoon Dijon mustard

1 cup candied walnuts, chopped

2 tablespoon extra-virgin olive oil

¼ cup feta cheese crumbles (optional)

¼ cup golden raisins

1 medium Pink Lady apple, peeled and chopped

½ teaspoon fresh cracked black pepper

¼ teaspoon kosher salt

2 bunches of kale, washed and dried

Preparation:

1. In a blender, add lemon juice, honey, garlic, shallot, vinegar, olive oil, salt, and pepper. Blend until smooth.

2. On a cutting board, chop up kale. In a large bowl, mix kale, apples, walnuts, raisins, and feta.

3. Pour on dressing and toss. Serve.

Note: If raw kale is too tough for you to cut, you can lightly stem and blanch in an ice bath before making this salad. You can also top this salad with any dried or fresh fruit you like. If you're vegan, omit cheese.

Arugula Crab Salad

Serves 4 // Time: 1 hour 15 minutes

Ingredients for Arugula Crab Salad

6 cups arugula, washed and dried

8 roasted red bell peppers or tomatoes, quartered slices

2 large eggs or egg whites

2 ½ tablespoon mayonnaise

1 ½ teaspoon Dijon mustard

1 teaspoon Worcestershire sauce

1 teaspoon Old Bay seasoning

¼ cup Parmesan cheese (more for optional topping)

1 teaspoon onion powder

1 teaspoon coriander

1 teaspoon garlic powder

4 lemons, quartered wedges

¼ teaspoon kosher salt

2 green onions, chopped

1 lbs. lump crab meat

2-3 cups Panko breadcrumbs

Light olive oil or canola oil for frying

Dressing of choice

Preparation:

1. Line a baking sheet with parchment paper for easy cleanup.

2. Combine the eggs, mayonnaise, green onion, Dijon mustard, Worcestershire sauce, Old Bay, and salt in a large bowl, mixing well. Check the crab meat for any hard or sharp cartilage.

3. Using a rubber spatula, add crab meat to the mixture, gently folding the mixture over the crab meat until all is combined. Be careful not to shred the crab meat as you do this.

4. Shape mixture into 8 cakes (each about ½ cup) and place on the prepared baking sheet. Cover and refrigerate for at least 25 minutes (This will help the crab cakes set).

5. In a shallow dish, combine Panko breadcrumbs and parmesan cheese. Cover each cake with the breadcrumbs, then place them on the lined baking sheet.

6. Preheat stove to medium-high heat and coat a large nonstick pan with olive oil. When the oil is hot, place the crab cakes in the pan and cook (3 to 5 minutes per side) until golden brown. Set crab cakes on paper towel to drain excess oil and cool.

7. Put arugula on a salad plate, top with roasted bell peppers and the crab cake. Sprinkle with parmesan cheese. Place lemon wedges on the side.

8. Use desired salad dressing. Serve immediately.

Grilled Chicken Caprese Salad with Avocado

Serves 4 // Time: 45 minutes

Ingredients for Salad

4 boneless, skinless chicken breasts
2 cup iceberg lettuce, washed and dried
3 cup romaine lettuce, washed and dried
2 medium tomatoes, diced
¾ cup mini bocconcini balls
¼ cup fresh basil leaves, thinly sliced

Ingredients for Marinade

2 teaspoon Splenda brown sugar
2 tablespoon basil pesto
¼ cup olive oil
Salt & pepper to season

Ingredients for Dressing

½ cup balsamic vinegar
1 tablespoon Splenda brown sugar
1 tablespoon Dijon mustard
1 shallot, minced
1 large garlic clove, minced
½ cup olive oil

½ teaspoon kosher salt

Preparation:

1. Marinade: In a bowl, combine brown sugar, basil pesto, olive oil, salt, and pepper. Put chicken in shallow dish and pour marinade over chicken, then cover with saran wrap. Refrigerate for 30 minutes. Remove chicken from marinade and pat dry with a paper towel.

2. Spray a grill pan (or large skillet) with nonstick spray and heat stove to medium. Add in chicken and season with salt and pepper. Cook for about 4 minutes on each side, or until chicken is cooked thoroughly.

3. In a small bowl, whisk together the balsamic vinegar, mustard, garlic, shallot, salt, and pepper. Add the oil and whisk thoroughly to combine. Continue whisking until the dressing is fully emulsified.

4. In a large serving bowl, mix iceberg and romaine lettuce. Slice chicken into strips.

5. Prepare salad with lettuce, sliced avocado, tomatoes, mozzarella cheese, and chicken. Top with basil strips; drizzle with the dressing.

Pescatarian-Friendly Caesar Cobb

Serves 2 // Time 30 minutes

Ingredients for Salad

2 large skinless salmon fillets
2 tablespoon lemon juice
1 teaspoon minced garlic
2 eggs, hard boiled and halved
3 cups romaine lettuce, chopped (washed and dried)
3 cups iceberg lettuce, chopped (washed and dried)
1 cup cherry or grape tomatoes, halved
1 avocado, diced
½ cup shaved parmesan cheese
1 cup cubed ciabatta
3 tablespoon freshly grated parmesan cheese
1 teaspoon garlic powder
1 teaspoon blackening seasoning
Olive oil for frying
Pinch of salt
Fresh cracked pepper for taste

Ingredients for Caesar Salad Dressing

¾ cup mayonnaise

3 tablespoon sour cream

1 ½ teaspoon anchovy paste

¼ cup olive oil

3 cloves of garlic, minced

1 tablespoon lemon juice a lemon

6 tablespoon freshly grated parmesan cheese

1 teaspoon Worcestershire sauce

Salt and pepper for seasoning

Preparation:

1. In a small bowl, whisk together all of the dressing ingredients until combined, then salt and pepper to taste. Refrigerate mixture.

2. Spread bread cubes on a parchment-lined baking sheet, then sprinkle with olive oil and grated parmesan cheese. Season with salt and pepper, then toss. Bake at 350 degrees until toasted about 10 minutes.

3. Season both sides of the salmon with garlic power, blackening seasoning, salt, and pepper. Coat a large skillet with olive oil. Fry salmon until golden on both sides and cooked to your liking.

4. In a large serving bowl, combine lettuce, avocado slices, shaved parmesan cheese, and croutons. Pour in the dressing and mix well to combine.

5. Finally, place the eggs and salmon on top of the salad and serve.

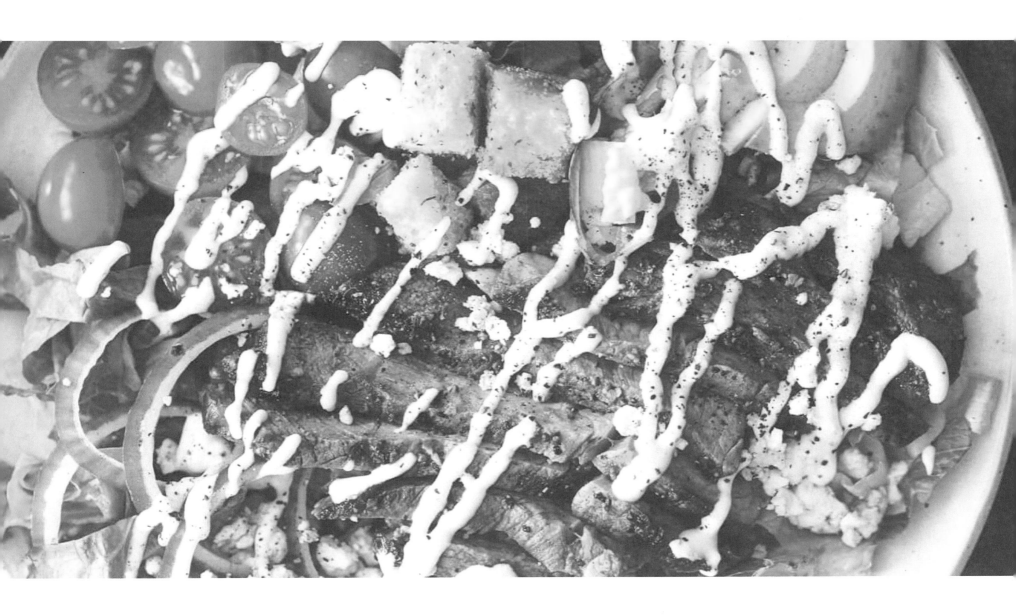

Black & Blue Teriyaki Steak Salad

Serves 4 // Time: 4 hours 25 minutes

Ingredients for Salad

2 boneless ribeye steak or sirloin (2 lbs. each)

6 cups spring mix greens, washed and dried

4 large portobello mushroom tops, wiped clean

⅓ cup blue cheese crumbles

½ cup cherry tomatoes, halved

1 avocado, thinly sliced

½ cup red onion, thinly sliced

3 tablespoon low sodium soy sauce

¼ cup orange juice

½ cup rice wine vinegar

2 tablespoon brown sugar

1 tablespoon minced garlic

1 teaspoon minced ginger

Salt and pepper for taste

Olive oil cooking spray

Salad dressing of choice

Croutons

Preparation

1. Put steak in a large Ziplock bag. In a small bowl, whisk soy sauce, orange juice, rice wine vinegar, brown sugar, black pepper, and garlic together. Pour mixture over steaks and let marinate in Ziplock bag for 4 hours or overnight.

2. Preheat grill. Take steaks out of the bag and pat dry with a paper towel. Season with salt and pepper, then drizzle with olive oil.

3. Put steaks on hot grill and cook until your desired likeness on both sides. Let steaks rest before slicing into thin strips.

4. Next, put l mushrooms on the grill, cook 5 mins on each side, remove and slice into strips.

5. In a large bowl, add spring mix, top with tomatoes, sliced avocado, and sliced onions. Put on steak and mushroom strips. Sprinkle blue cheese crumbles and fried onions on top and serve.

The 3 "S" Salad with Warm Bacon Vinaigrette

Serves 4 // Time: 30 minutes

Ingredients for Salad

24 medium shrimp, peeled and deveined
2 tablespoon melted butter
10 cups fresh spinach, washed and dried
¼ cup sundried tomatoes
½ cup red onion, sliced
½ cup almonds, sliced
½ teaspoon garlic powder
½ teaspoon olive oil
¼ teaspoon onion powder
¼ teaspoon cayenne pepper (optional)
¼ teaspoon coriander
¼ teaspoon lemon herb old bay
¼ teaspoon paprika
¼ teaspoon granulated sugar
1 teaspoon freshly ground black pepper
1 teaspoon kosher salt

Ingredients for Dressing

½ cup light olive oil

4 slices bacon, cooked and minced

¼ cup red wine vinegar

1 shallot, minced

½ cup cornstarch

¼ cup granulated sugar

1 ½ teaspoon Dijon mustard

¼ teaspoon salt

¼ teaspoon coarse ground black pepper

Preparation:

1. Preheat grill. Toss shrimp with olive oil in a bowl. In another small bowl, combine garlic, onion powder, coriander, lemon herb old bay, paprika, salt, and pepper. Sprinkle mixture over shrimp, coating both sides. Spray grill with cooking spray and grill shrimp until done.

2. Dressing: In a small bowl, whisk together all the ingredients, except olive oil. Once completed, whisk in olive oil slowly until combined. Set aside.

3. In a large serving bowl, add spinach, tomatoes, red onions, shrimp, and almonds. Toss to combine.

4. Put dressing in microwave for 30 seconds, whisk to combine, then pour dressing over salad.

5. Toss everything together and serve.

Chapter 2

SOUPS

Butternut Squash Soup with Crème

Ingredients for Soup

3 medium butternut squash, cubed

2 tablespoon olive oil, more for drizzle

1 small onion, diced

2 stalks celery, chopped

1 orange bell pepper, chopped

1 medium carrot, chopped

1 small sweet potato, chopped

½ teaspoon chicken bouillon

4 cups chicken stock

1 tablespoon thyme

1 teaspoon salt

1 teaspoon black pepper

4 slices cooked bacon, chopped (optional)

2 tablespoon heavy whipping cream

1 teaspoon freshly ground nutmeg

¼ cup crème fraîche

¼ cup chives, thinly chopped

Preparation:

1. Preheat oven to 375°F. On a baking sheet, spread squash and sweet potatoes. Drizzle with olive oil and salt and pepper. Toss to combine and bake until squash is fork-tender.

2. Heat a large Dutch oven to medium heat. Add onions, celery, carrots, thyme, salt, and pepper. Cook until vegetables have softened. Add chicken stock and bouillon. Let soup simmer for 20 minutes, stirring occasionally.

3. Puree soup with an immersion blender, or transfer to a blender until smooth. If soup is not thick enough, let simmer until desired thickness.

4. In a small bowl, combine whipping cream, nutmeg, and crème fraiche.

5. Serve soup in a bowl with a dollop of the crème fraiche mixture in the center, top with bacon and chives.

Hamburger Soup with Ditalini Pasta

Serves 4// Time: 50 minutes

Ingredients for Soup

1 lbs. ground beef

4 tablespoon olive oil, halved

1 red peppers, diced

3 stacks of celery, chopped

1 large onion, diced

¼ cup white wine

1 pk. frozen green beans (canned is okay, but rinse twice)

28 oz. canned peeled tomatoes

4 cloves of garlic, sliced

1 tablespoon tomatoes paste

1 cup ditalini pasta

1 bay leaf

3 sprigs of fresh thyme

4 cups beef stock

1 cup water

1 teaspoon beef bouillon

1 teaspoon dry oregano

Salt and pepper to taste

Preparation:

1. Heat a large Dutch oven on medium heat. Add 2 tablespoons of olive oil and the ground beef. (Make sure to crumble the beef as it cooks.) When beef has browned, pour it into a colander lined with paper towels to drain excess oil.

2. Drizzle more olive oil into Dutch oven. Add in onions and cook until softened. Add in garlic and stir until fragrant. Deglaze with wine to deglaze and reduce to half.

3. Add in vegetables, beef stock, bouillon, and beef into win mixture. Cook for about 20 minutes. Add in pasta and let cook for another 4-8 minutes or until pasta is softened.

4. Salt and pepper to taste.

5. Serve warm.

Cajun Smoked Turkey and Bean Soup

Serves 6 // Time: 1 hour 25 minutes

Ingredients for Soup

1 lb. Great Northern beans, sorted and soaked overnight

1 lb. smoked turkey breast, leftover turkey, or smoked turkey sausage, diced

2 tablespoon olive oil

1 small onion, diced

2 stalks celery, chopped

2 cups kale leaves, chopped

3 tablespoon heavy cream (optional)

3 medium white sweet potatoes, washed and cubed with skin

1 medium carrot, chopped

¼ teaspoon Cajun seasoning

6 cloves of garlic, minced

½ teaspoon chicken bouillon

4 cup chicken stock

4 sprigs of fresh thyme

1 teaspoon ground cumin

1 teaspoon kosher salt

2 tablespoon crushed red pepper (optional)

1 teaspoon black pepper

Preparation:

1. Heat olive oil in a large Dutch oven over medium heat. Add in onion, celery, and carrots. Sauté until vegetables soften, then add garlic, Cajun seasoning, salt, and pepper. (If you are using smoked turkey sausage, add it in now and sauté with vegetables.)

2. Add turkey wings or leftover turkey, beans, cumin, thyme, chicken stock, and bouillon into Dutch oven. Bring to boil about 2-3 minutes and then reduce heat. Let simmer for 1 ½ hours, stirring occasionally.

3. In about an hour, check to see if turkey is fork-tender. Remove turkey and let cool.

4. When meat is cool, remove the meat from the bone in large pieces. Add meat back to the soup. Remove thyme sprigs. Add in kale, heavy whipping cream, and crushed red peppers. Let simmer for 5 minutes.

5. Serve warm with cornbread or hot water cornbread.

Creamy Potatoes & Sausage Soup with Kale (A.K.A. Zuppa)

Serves 6-8 // Time: 50 minutes

Ingredients for Soup

1 lbs. Italian sausage, spicy or mild

2 tablespoon olive oil

2 tablespoon butter

1 large onion, diced

5-6 cloves of garlic, minced

4 cup chicken stock

½ tablespoon chicken bouillon

½ cup white wine

4 large russet potatoes, scrubbed and sliced with skin on

1 teaspoon crushed red pepper flakes (optional)

4 cups kale leaves, roughly chopped, no stems

1 cup heavy whipping cream

2 tablespoon cornstarch (optional)

1 teaspoon crushed red pepper

¼ cup freshly grated parmesan cheese

3 slices of pancetta, cooked and crumbled

Preparation:

1. Heat a large Dutch oven on medium-high heat. Add 2 tablespoons of olive oil and then sausage, making sure to crumble the sausage as it cooks.

When sausage has browned, pour into a colander lined with paper towels to drain excess oil.

2. Put pot back on the heat, add butter and then onions. Cook onions until softened, then add garlic, stirring until fragrant. Next, add potatoes, chicken stock, bouillon, red pepper flakes, and sausage.

Bring to a gentle boil for about 15-25 minutes until potatoes are tender.

3. In a cup, mix cornstarch with heavy whipping cream. Drizzle into pot, slowly stirring. Add kale leaves and cook for another 3 minutes Salt and pepper to taste.

4. Serve warm and top with pancetta and freshly grated parmesan cheese

Super Simple, Creamy Chicken Tortellini Stew

Serves 4 // Time: 30 minutes

Ingredients for Soup

1 rotisserie chicken, shredded

1 pk. cheese tortellini,

2 tablespoon olive oil

¼ teaspoon nutmeg, freshly grated

1 small onion, diced

2 celery stalks, chopped

¼ teaspoon crushed red pepper (optional)

2 cups heavy cream or milk, plus 2 tablespoon

1 cup frozen peas, rinsed and thaw

1 medium carrot, chopped

3 garlic cloves, minced

½ teaspoon chicken bouillon

4 cups chicken stock

1 teaspoon dry oregano

1 teaspoon kosher salt

1 teaspoon black pepper

1 ½ tablespoon corn starch

Freshly grated parmesan for garnish

Preparation:

1. Put a large Dutch oven over medium heat and add olive oil. Add in onion, celery, and carrots. Sauté vegetables until they soften, then add garlic, red pepper, salt, and pepper.

2. Add chicken, tortellini, chicken stock, and bouillon to the Dutch oven.

3. Bring to boil about 2-3 minutes and then reduce heat. Let simmer for half an hour, stirring occasionally.

4. In a small bowl, mix corn starch and 2 tablespoons of heavy whipping cream. Slowly drizzle cream into pot while stirring. Then, add the rest of the heavy whipping cream, nutmeg, and peas. Let simmer for 10 minutes.

5. When ready to serve, ladle stew into a bowl and top with freshly grated parmesan.

Delightful Corn Chowder

Serves 6 // Time: 50 minutes

Ingredients for Soup

3 ears of corn, shucked

2 cups frozen corn

¾ cup heavy whipping cream

2 tablespoon olive oil, more for drizzle

1 small onion, diced

2 celery stalks, chopped

1 red bell pepper, chopped

3 medium Korean sweet potatoes, washed and cubed with skin

1 medium carrot, chopped

¼ teaspoon cayenne pepper

2 garlic cloves, minced

1 bay leaf

½ teaspoon chicken bouillon

4 cups chicken stock

1 tablespoon thyme

1 teaspoon kosher salt

1 teaspoon black pepper

2 tablespoon chives, thinly chopped

½ teaspoon slurry (optional - ½ teaspoon corn starch and ½ teaspoon water)

Preparation:

1. Cut the kernels from the cobs. Scrape down the cobbs for the corn milk or juices, then set kernels aside.

2. Heat a large Dutch oven to medium heat, then add onion, celery, and carrots. Season vegetables with salt and pepper to taste and cook for 3 minutes. Then, add garlic and cook for another minute. Add corn, sweet potatoes, bell pepper, thyme, bay leaf, chicken stock, and bouillon.

3. Bring to a boil, then reduce heat and let soup simmer for 15 minutes, stirring occasionally until sweet potatoes are fork tender.

4. Remove bay leaf. Stir in heavy cream, cayenne pepper, and salt and pepper to taste. If soup isn't thick enough, add slurry to thicken. Let simmer for 3 minutes to thicken.

5. Serve with sprinkles of chives on top.

Jamaican Chicken Soup

Serves 6 // Time: 1 hour 5 minutes

Ingredients for Soup

3 lbs. boneless, skinless chicken breast and thighs, chopped into large cubes

3 ears of corn, sliced

3 carrots, large, chopped at an angle

1 medium chayote (cho-cho), chopped into large chunks

2 large green onions, sliced on an angle

1 red pepper, diced

1 large onion, diced

4 garlic cloves, sliced

1 whole scotch bonnet (optional)

3 large potatoes, diced

3 sprigs fresh thyme

8-10 cups water

1 medium buttercup squash (or pumpkin), diced in large pieces

1 medium Jamaican yam (or butternut squash), diced largely

1 pk. Grace Caribbean Cock Soup (spicy pimento flavor)

1 can of chicken noodle soup

1 teaspoon chicken bouillon

Ingredients for Dumplings

¼ cup cornmeal

1 cup flour

½ teaspoon salt

Warm water

Room temperature butter

Preparation:

1. For Dumplings: mix the flour and cornmeal together with a dusting of salt. Add a little warm water at a time until a soft dough forms. Set aside for 10 minutes. Take about a tablespoon dough and roll into medium-sized sphere shape then drop into boiling soup.

2. In a large stock pot, bring 4 cups of water to a boil and add buttercup squash, thyme, and chicken. Cover and cook on high for 10 minutes. Then, add dumplings. Cover and cook covered, stirring occasionally for 5 minutes.

3. Add another 4 cups water to the pot. Bring the pot back to boil, add bell pepper, chayote, carrots, corn, onion, garlic, potatoes, yam, and bouillon. Cook covered for 20 minutes, stirring occasionally. If vegetables are still hard, add in 2 more cups of water. Add in chicken noodle soup and scotch bonnet. Cook for about 10-15 minutes with the pot covered and stir occasionally.

4. Serve hot. Garnish with thinly sliced green onions.

Grandmother's Hearty Vegetable Soup

Serves 6-8 // Time: 55 minutes

Ingredients for Soup

1 medium butternut squash, diced

1 red pepper, diced

3 celery stalks, chopped

1 large onion, diced

1 pk. frozen mixed vegetables, (corn, carrots, and green beans)

1 pk. frozen okra

1 can of diced tomatoes

4 garlic cloves, sliced

2 cups kale leaves, cabbage, or baby spinach, chopped

3 potatoes, large diced

3 sprigs fresh thyme

4 cup beef stock

1 teaspoon beef bouillon

½ teaspoon Creole seasoning

¼ teaspoon cayenne pepper (optional)

1 teaspoon dry oregano

Salt and pepper to taste

Preparation:

1. Put a large Dutch oven over medium heat. Add olive oil, onion, celery, and carrots. Sauté vegetables until they soften, then add garlic, cook until fragrant, adding in red pepper, salt, and pepper.

2. Add the remainder of the ingredients. Bring Dutch oven to a boil, reduce heat, and let simmer for 45 minutes, stirring occasionally.

3. Serve warm with a muffin or slice of buttered bread.

Chapter 3

SIDE DISHES

Dill Zucchini and Squash

Serves 4-6 // Time: 30 minutes

Ingredients for Side Dish

1 medium zucchini, sliced

1 medium yellow squash, sliced

1 red bell pepper, diced

1 small onion, diced

2 garlic cloves, minced

2 tablespoon butter

2 tablespoon olive oil

1 teaspoon fresh dill, or dried

Salt and pepper

Preparation:

1. Heat skillet on medium heat. Drizzle in olive oil and add diced onions.

2. Sauté until the onions soften.

3. Add garlic and sauté for about 3 minutes until fragrant.

4. Add bell peppers, zucchini, squash and dill. Season with salt and pepper and sauté until all vegetables have softened.

5. Add butter and toss mixture until melted.

6. Serve.

Easy Pleasy Broccoli and Corn

Serves 6-8 // Time: 50 minutes

Ingredients for Dish

24 oz. frozen corn

14 oz. frozen broccoli

2 oz. shredded Velveeta cheese

2 oz. triple cheddar cheese

¾ cup heavy cream

3-4 slices of breadcrumbs(optional)

4 oz. cream cheese

9 tablespoon butter

Salt and Pepper

Preparation:

1. Preheat oven to 350 degrees F. Lightly butter a 9-inch baking dish and set aside.

2. In a skillet, melt butter and add breadcrumbs to lightly toast. Remove from heat.

3. In a saucepan on medium heat, add in cream cheese, heavy cream, and ½ stick of butter. Stir until cream cheese is melted, then promptly remove from heat.

4. Place half of the corn into the buttered baking dish and spread out evenly.

5. Spread half of the broccoli on top of the corn. Next, spread half of the cream cheese mixture over the broccoli and corn. Sprinkle on half of the Velveeta cheese and the triple cheddar cheese.

6. Repeat layering with the remaining corn, broccoli, cream cheese mixture, and shredded cheese. Top with toasted breadcrumbs.

7. Bake the dish for about 40-50 minutes until everything is heated through and the top layer is golden brown.

8. Serve hot

Parmesan Brussels Sprouts with Balsamic Reduction

Serves 4 // Time: 30 minutes

Ingredients for Brussels Sprouts

1 lb. brussels sprouts, trimmed and halved
1 tablespoon Cajun season
1 teaspoon garlic powder
1 teaspoon onion powder
4 garlic cloves, diced
1 small onion, diced
2 tablespoon olive oil plus more for drizzle
4 tablespoon butter
Salt and freshly coarse black pepper
3 tablespoon parmesan cheese, freshly grated
Olive oil cooking spray

Ingredients for Balsamic Reduction

2 cups balsamic vinegar
¼ cup sugar
¼ cup brown sugar

Preparation:

1. Preheat oven to 375° F. Spray baking sheet with cooking spray.

2. For brussels sprouts: Put brussels sprouts, garlic powder, onion powder, Cajun seasoning, salt, and pepper in a large bowl.

3. Drizzle with olive oil and toss to combine. Spread onto baking sheet with the cut side down. Bake until tender, or for about 30 minutes.

4. For Balsamic Reduction: Heat balsamic vinegar and sugars on medium-high heat in a medium saucepan. Bring pot to a gentle boil, then reduce heat to low. Let mixture simmer, stirring occasionally, until the vinegar thickens and is reduced to half about 20 mins. It should be thick enough to coat the back of a spoon. Remove mixture from heat and allow to cool completely before serving.

5. While brussels sprouts is still hot, grate parmesan cheese over the top and toss.

6. Put in a baking dish grate a little more parmesan and drizzle balsamic sauce over.

7. Serve hot.

Perfectly Seasoned Collard Greens with Smoked Turkey

Serves 6-8 // Time: 31 hours 45 minutes

Ingredients for Dish

2-3 bunches of collard greens, stems removed, washed and chopped roughly

4 cups chicken broth, homemade is the best

3 tablespoon apple cider vinegar

1 red bell pepper, diced

1 green bell pepper, diced

4 garlic cloves, minced

2 onions, diced

1-2 teaspoon granulated garlic

1 pk. smoked turkey neck

1 small pk. smoked turkey wing drumettes

1 tablespoon chicken bouillon

1 teaspoon crushed red pepper

kosher salt

coarse black pepper

1 cup water

Preparation:

1. Heat a large stock pot on medium heat. Add chicken stock, half of the onions, the bell pepper, garlic, and turkey, then salt and pepper to season. Bring pot up to a gentle boil until turkey meat is fork tender, then remove drumettes.

2. When the drumettes are cool, remove the meat from bone and chop, then set aside.

3. Taste the broth. This is the 1st adjustment to the seasoning. Add vinegar, bouillon, and crushed red pepper, then stir.

4. Bring broth back to a boil. Add half of the greens, then add turkey. Stir in 1 teaspoon of garlic and the onion. Add in the remainder of the greens. The water from the greens will add more broth. Cover and let the water from the greens reduce. Stir to make sure all the greens are submerged in broth.

5. Reduce heat to simmer and let greens cook for 45 minutes to hour until done, stirring occasionally.

6. Check to make sure you have enough broth. If not, add more water. Perform the 2nd taste test and adjust with garlic, salt, and pepper. Add 2 tablespoons of sugar during the 2nd tasting to add more definition to the greens.

7. Serve while hot with a tomato and onion salad and hot water cornbread.

Note: Instructions on how to clean and chop greens can be found on page 70 and 71.

Savory Sweet Potatoes Mash

Serves 6 // Time: 40 minutes

Ingredients for Dish

3 medium sweet potatoes, peeled and diced

3 medium white sweet potatoes, peeled and diced

½ cup heavy cream

1 small onion, grated

4 tablespoon butter

2 tablespoon brown sugar

1 teaspoon vanilla

½ teaspoon parsley, dried and freshly chopped

1 bay leaf

2 garlic cloves, minced

2 tablespoon olive oil

1 teaspoon salt

1 teaspoon pepper

freshly grated nutmeg

water

Preparation:

1. In a large pot, boil water with a bay leaf and add in potatoes. Boil until potatoes are fork tender. Pour into strainer to drain and remove bay leaf, then set aside.

2. Heat pot to medium-high. Drizzle in olive oil and sauté onion until it softens. Add garlic and sauté until fragrant. Turn off heat.

3. Add in sweet potatoes and mash with onion and garlic to combine.

4. Turn on heat to medium, then add in cream, parsley, vanilla, sugar, and butter. Add salt and pepper to taste.

5. Top with freshly grated nutmeg and serve hot.

Simple Green Beans with Lemon Butter Sauce

Serves 4 // Time: 30 minutes

Ingredients for Dish

3 lbs. green beans, washed and trimmed

4 garlic cloves, minced

1 small onion, diced

2 tablespoon olive oil

3 tablespoon unsalted butter

½ small lemon

salt

fresh cracked black pepper or coarse black pepper

Preparation:

1. Bring about a cup of water to boil. Place green beans in a steam basket and put it over the boiling water. Let green beans steam for about 3 minutes, or until beans are soft but still firm. Steam for a shorter time or longer, depending on your desired doneness.

2. Put basket immediately into an ice water bath to stop the cooking. Remove and let drain.

3. In the meantime, put a large skillet on medium heat. Add olive oil and onions, then season with salt and pepper. Sauté until softened. Add garlic sauté until fragrant.

4. Add butter and green beans, covering green beans with garlic butter and onion until warmed.

5. Squeeze lemon juice over green beans, toss, and add salt and pepper to taste.

6. Serve immediately.

Tomato & Onion Salad with Hot Water Cornbread

Serves 4 // Time: 1 hour 30 minutes

Ingredients for Salad

2 medium vine ripe tomatoes, sliced

2 medium sweet onions, halved and sliced

½ cup apple cider vinegar

2 tablespoon garlic cloves, diced

1 tablespoon sugar

1 teaspoon season salt

1 teaspoon coarse black pepper

Ingredients for Cornbread

2 teaspoon sugar

1 cup boiling hot water

2 cup white self-rising cornmeal

1 teaspoon seasoning salt

2 tablespoon melted butter

2 teaspoon garlic cloves, minced

¼ cup onion, grated

1 teaspoon black pepper

Canola or peanut oil for frying

Preparation:

1. For the salad: In a large glass dish, overlap tomatoes slices and onion slices, then top with garlic cloves.

2. In a measuring cup, combine apple cider vinegar with sugar, salt, and pepper. Pour over the tomatoes, onion, and garlic, then cover.

3. Refrigerate overnight before serving.

4. For the cornbread: In a small bowl, mix cornmeal, onion, garlic, salt, pepper, and sugar.

5. Add boiling water to the bowl and stir until everything has thickened and combined.

6. Pour enough oil to coat a large, nonstick skillet and heat at medium-high heat.

7. When the oil is hot enough for frying, drop a tablespoon spoonful of the mixture into the oil and flatten slightly. Fry each cornbread until brown and crisp. Using a spatula, flip to the other side and cook for about 3-5 minutes, or until brown.

8. Remove and place on paper towels to drain.

9. Serve immediately.

Yum Stovetop Mac & Cheese

Serves 6-8 // Time: 20 minutes

Ingredients for Dish

8 oz. elbow macaroni pasta

1 cup Velveeta cheese, cubed

1 cup mild cheddar cheese, freshly grated

1 cup sharp cheddar cheese, freshly grated

½ cup parmesan cheese, freshly grated

6 tablespoon unsalted butter

1 teaspoon season salt or accent

1 teaspoon black pepper

½ teaspoon garlic powder (optional)

3 cups milk

1 cup heavy cream

¼ cup flour

¼ teaspoon nutmeg

Olive oil

Salt and pepper to taste

Preparation:

1. Cook macaroni in heavily salted, boiling water until al dente. Drain and rinse macaroni. Lightly drizzle olive oil over macaroni and toss to prevent from sticking, then set aside.

2. In a large bowl, mix together cheeses and set aside.

3. In large Dutch oven on medium-high heat, melt butter and whisk in flour. Let cook for a minute until mixture turns a golden-brown color.

4. Gradually, whisk in cream and milk until smooth, then whisk in garlic powder and nutmeg. Season with salt and pepper.

5. Stir in cheese until blended. Next, stir in macaroni until combined.

6. Serve hot.

Chapter 4

MAIN DISHES

Cajun Fried Pork

Serves 4 // Time: 30 minutes

2 tablespoon olive oil
1 tablespoon dry thyme
1 teaspoon basil
¼ cup white wine
3 garlic cloves, minced
1 tablespoon Cajun seasoning
1 teaspoon garlic powder
1 teaspoon onion powder
kosher salt
coarse black pepper

Preparation:

1. Season pork with Cajun seasoning, garlic powder, onion powder, salt, and pepper.

2. Heat large skillet on high. Add olive oil and sear pork chops on both sides. Remove once browned.

3. Deglaze with white wine. Let wine reduce to half. Bring heat to medium-low.

4. Add pork chops back in skillet. Top with onions, mushrooms, thyme, and basil. Season with salt and pepper.

5. Cover skillet and let cook for about 20 minutes or until chops are fork tender. To prevent burning, check both sides and scrape bottom of skillet.

6. Remove lid and let the juices evaporate, let pork chops get a nice crust on the bottom. Let onion get brown and move to the top of the pork chops to prevent burning.

7. Serve hot with rice or a side of your choice.

Ingredients for Dish
4 pork chops
2 cups button mushroom tops
3 large onions, sliced

Cajun Swai Fish with Lemon Butter Caper Sauce

Serves 4 // Time: 20 minutes

Ingredients for Dish

4 pieces of Swai fish or flounder

1 teaspoon smoked paprika

½ teaspoon cumin

½ teaspoon coriander

1 teaspoon Cajun seasoning

1 teaspoon garlic powder

1 small onion, diced

1 teaspoon kosher salt

1 teaspoon coarse black pepper

2 teaspoon brown sugar (optional)

1 teaspoon dry oregano

4 garlic cloves, chopped

3 tablespoon capers, rinsed and drained

3 tablespoon lemon juice, freshly squeezed

4 tablespoon butter, cold

Olive oil

Preparation:

1. In a small bowl, combine paprika, cumin, coriander, Cajun seasoning, garlic powder, onion powder, brown sugar, salt, and pepper.

2. Rinse fish, then sprinkle both sides with seasoning mix.

3. In a large skillet heat on high heat, add olive oil and fry fish until done. About 1 ½ minutes per side. Remove to a plate.

4. In a large skillet on medium heat, add olive oil and onions. Sauté until softened. Add garlic and sauté until fragrant. Then, add capers and lemon juice. Cook for about 1 minute until garlic softens a bit.

5. Remove from heat. Add 2 tablespoons of butter at a time to the caper sauce, stirring until butter melts and forms a creamy mixture.

6. Add fish back to the pan and spoon sauce over the fish.

7. Serve hot.

Chicken Alfredo with Broccoli

Serves 4 // Time: 2 hours 35 minutes

Ingredients for Dish

2 cups frozen broccoli crowns, thawed and rinsed

4 skinless, boneless chicken breasts

1 ½ teaspoon garlic powder

1 ½ teaspoon onion powder

¼ cup marsala wine

½ teaspoon seasoned salt

1 ½ teaspoon cumin

1 ½ teaspoon paprika

1 ½ teaspoon Creole seasoning

1 teaspoon kosher salt

1 ½ teaspoon black pepper

1 cup Pecorino Romano cheese, freshly grated

1 cup parmesan cheese, freshly grated

1 pk. Pappardelle or fettuccine noodles

1 cup heavy cream

1 cup milk

4-6 garlic cloves, minced

2 tablespoon flour

½ teaspoon nutmeg, freshly grated

3 tablespoon butter

2 tablespoon fresh parsley, chopped

¼ cup olive oil, plus more for drizzling

Preparation:

1. In a small mixing bowl, combine onion powder, garlic powder, cumin, paprika, seasoned salt, Creole seasoning, and black pepper.

2. Put chicken in a large Ziplock bag. Add olive oil, marsala, and half of the seasoning from the mixing bowl. Seal and let chicken marinate for 2 hours in refrigerator.

3. Remove from refrigerator and put on paper towel to drain and pat dry. Set aside.

4. Preheat grill. Drizzle chicken with oil and season on both sides with the remainder of the seasoning mix. Grill each side for 5-8 minutes until done. Let rest for 5 minutes, then slice into strips.

5. In boiling water, cook pasta in heavily salted water until al dente. Drain and rinse pasta then lightly drizzle olive oil over and toss to prevent from sticking. Set aside.

6. In a large Dutch oven on medium-high heat, melt butter and add garlic sauté until fragrant, then whisk in flour. Let mixture cook for a minute until it turns a golden-brown color.

7. Gradually, whisk in cream and milk until smooth. Add nutmeg and season with salt and pepper.

8. Stir in cheese until blended. Add pasta and broccoli, stirring to combined. Add salt and pepper to taste.

9. Put grilled chicken on top. Garnish with parsley.

10. Serve hot with garlic bread.

Creamy Spinach Stuffed Salmon

Serves 4 // Time: 30 minutes

Ingredients for Dish

24 oz. skinless salmon

1 red bell pepper, sliced

1 yellow bell pepper, sliced

2 garlic cloves, chopped

1 large onion, sliced

4-6 tablespoon unsalted butter

½ cup Panko breadcrumbs

16 oz. frozen spinach, squeezed

½ cup cream cheese, room temperature

1 pk. vegetable mix

1 cup mayonnaise

3 teaspoon garlic cloves, minced

1 teaspoon garlic powder

1 teaspoon black ground pepper

1 teaspoon onion powder

1 teaspoon coriander

1 teaspoon Cajun seasoning

½ lemon

2 tablespoon parmesan cheese, freshly grated

Preparation:

1. Preheat oven at 375° F.

2. In a large bowl, mix spinach, cream cheese, vegetable, mayonnaise, and minced garlic. Stir until combined and set aside.

3. Using a sharp knife, butterfly the salmon fillet by cutting half-way through the side of the fillet. Stuff the center with the spinach mixture.

4. In a large glass baking dish, put the bell pepper, chopped garlic, and onions on the bottom of the dish. Top with butter, salt, and pepper. Put the salmon on top and squeeze the lemon over the top.

5. In a small bowl, combine garlic powder, black pepper, onion powder, coriander, Cajun seasoning, and salt.

6. Sprinkle the seasoning mixture on top of the salmon. Then top with parmesan cheese, then Panko breadcrumbs. Drizzle with olive oil.

7. Bake the stuffed fillets for about 15-20 minutes, depending on how large your fillets are.

8. Serve warm.

Grilled Lamb Chops with Apricot Mint Balsamic

Serves 6 // Time: 8 hours 30 minutes

Ingredients for Lamb Chops

6 lamb chops, ¾-inch thick, washed

4 garlic cloves, chopped

2 cups milk

¼ cup balsamic vinegar

1 teaspoon dry rosemary

1 teaspoon dry thyme

2 teaspoon kosher salt, plus 1 teaspoon

1 teaspoon coarse black pepper

1 teaspoon crushed red pepper

Olive oil

1 teaspoon garlic powder

1 teaspoon seasoned salt

Ingredients for Balsamic

2 cups balsamic vinegar

3 tablespoon apricot preserves

2 garlic cloves, minced

¼ cup brown sugar

2 tablespoon fresh mint, chopped

Preparation:

1. In a large Ziplock bag, add lamb chops, milk, chopped garlic, balsamic, rosemary, and thyme. Put in 2 teaspoons of salt, crushed red pepper, and olive oil. Seal bag and toss lamb in mixture. Let marinade for 8 hours or overnight. Remove and put on paper towel to pat dry. Let chops warm to room temperature.

2. For Balsamic: In a medium saucepan on medium heat, add the balsamic vinegar and sugars. Bring to a gentle boil, then reduce heat to low. Let simmer, stirring occasionally, until the vinegar thickens, and the mixture reduces to half. It should be thick enough to coat the back of a spoon. Remove from the heat and allow to completely cool before serving.

3. Preheat grill. Season chops with seasoned salt, garlic powder, black pepper, and kosher salt on both sides. Drizzle with olive oil.

4. Put the chops on the grill and brush with balsamic glaze. Cook to medium-rare or to your liking.

5. Serve warm.

Pot Roast with Root Vegetables

Serves 6 // Time: 4 hours 30 minutes

Ingredients for Dish

3-4 lbs. chuck roast

2 large carrots, diced in large chunks

2 large parsnips, diced in large chunks

1 bay leaf

2 tablespoon olive oil

2 tablespoon butter

4 red potatoes, washed and cut into 4 pieces

6 garlic cloves, chopped

2 white sweet potatoes, diced in large chunks

2 celery ribs, chop into 1-inch pieces

3 fresh thyme sprigs

2 teaspoon dry rosemary

2 large onions, diced in large chunks

1 teaspoon granulated garlic

1 teaspoon ground ginger

1 teaspoon granulated onion

1 red bell pepper, sliced and halved

1 green bell pepper, sliced and halved

¼ teaspoon cayenne pepper

½ teaspoon coarse black pepper

½ cup sweet marsala wine

2 tablespoon Worcestershire sauce

4 cups beef stock

1 tablespoon beef bouillon

2-3 tablespoon cornstarch

2 tablespoon water

Salt and pepper to taste

Thinly sliced chives (optional to garnish)

Preparation:

1. Preheat oven to 350°F.

2. Season pot roast with granulated garlic, granulated onion, salt, and pepper on all sides. Put a large Dutch oven on high heat and drizzle in olive oil. Add the beef, searing on both sides. Once the meat has browned, remove and set aside.

3. Reduce the heat to medium. Add butter, then half of the onion. Sauté until the onion has softened. Add garlic and cook until fragrant.

4. Deglaze pan with marsala wine. Let the liquid reduces to half. Add beef, thyme, ginger, cayenne, rosemary, beef stock, Worcestershire and bouillon. Cover and let bake for 3-4 hours, or until fork tender.

5. Add in all the vegetables, and cover let bake for about 15 mins until vegetables are tender.

6. Remove pan from oven and carefully pour in half of the broth into a glass bowl. Then set pan aside.

7. In a small bowl, combine cornstarch and water, then whisk in the broth.

8. Pour mixture over the meat and vegetables. Gently toss to mix. Cover and put back in the oven.

9. Bake for about 15-20 minutes until vegetables are fork tender.

10. Garnish with chives or parsley. Serve hot with a dinner roll or cornbread.

Rockin Red Beans and Rice with Andouille Sausage

Serves 6-8 // Time: 1 hour

Ingredients for Dish

2 medium onion

1 yellow bell pepper, diced

1 red bell pepper, diced

1 green bell pepper, diced

4 slices of bacon, chopped

2 stalks of celery, diced

4 garlic cloves, chopped

1 teaspoon garlic powder

2 teaspoon tomato paste

1 teaspoon onion powder

1 teaspoon Cajun seasoning

1 teaspoon cayenne pepper (optional)

1 teaspoon crushed red pepper (optional)

1 pk. smoked turkey or pork andouille sausage, sliced

½ cup fresh parsley, chopped

1 teaspoon kosher salt

1 teaspoon black pepper

3 sprigs fresh thyme

4 bay leaves

1 lb. red beans, picked and soaked

4 cups chicken stock, vegetable stock or water

1 tablespoon chicken bouillon

1 green onion, sliced (optional for garnish)

white rice, cooked

Olive oil cooking spray

Preparation:

1. Rinse dry beans and pick through, discarding any foreign objects. Add beans to a large pot and cover with 3-4 inches of cold water. Let the beans sit overnight.

2. Drain the soaked beans, rinse them, and set aside.

3. Spray a large Dutch oven with cooking spray and heat it on high. Cook bacon until it browns. Remove it promptly and let it drain on paper towels.

4. Leave about 1 tablespoon of bacon fat in the pot and add sausage and Tasso. Add onion and garlic to the pot and sauté with sausage. Let cook for about 3-5 minutes, or until meat is brown, and onion and garlic are fragrant.

5. Next, stir in all the remaining vegetables, beans, chicken stock, bouillon, bay leaf, thyme, and seasonings.

6. Bring mixture to a boil 2 to 3 minutes and reduce heat to low. Let simmer for 1 ½ hours, stirring occasionally until beans are tender. Remove bay leaves and stems. Salt and pepper to taste.

7. Serve hot over rice and topped with green onions.

Notes: If you like the sauce to be a little thicker, mix 2 tablespoons of corn starch with 2 tablespoons of water, then slowly mixt into pot. For vegan options remove the sausages and use vegetable broth or water.

Spicy Fried Chicken

Serves 5-10 // Time: 4 hours 35 minutes

Ingredients for Dish

10 pieces of mixed chicken, clean (breast, wings, legs, and thighs with skin on)

3-4 cups flour

1 ½ cups cornstarch

¼ cup hot sauce

2 teaspoon Cajun seasoning or Creole seasoning

2 teaspoon cayenne pepper

2 teaspoon garlic powder

2 teaspoon onion powder

1 teaspoon dry mustard

2 teaspoon season salt

2 teaspoon smoked paprika

1 teaspoon ground ginger

6-8 cups peanut oil or canola oil

2 teaspoon black pepper

2 t. chili powder

2-3 cup buttermilk

2 eggs

4 garlic cloves, crushed

1 teaspoon ground herb mix (thyme, basil, and oregano)

Salt

Preparation:

1. In a large bowl, add chicken, a handful of kosher salt, crushed garlic, and fill with enough water to submerge the chicken. Cover and refrigerate for 4 hours or overnight, preferably. Drain and disregard garlic cloves.

2. In a large bowl, whisk flour, cornstarch, cayenne pepper, onion powder, garlic powder, dry mustard, herbs, paprika, and chili powder together until combined. Set aside.

3. In a large bowl, whisk buttermilk, hot sauce, Cajun seasoning, and eggs together. Add chicken and toss to cover all pieces.

4. Coat chicken in flour mixture. shake to remove excess flour on wire rack. Let the chicken rest for about 10 minutes while preparing oil.

5. In a large Dutch oven, heat oil on high heat to 350°F, using a frying thermometer.

6. Fry 2-3 pieces of chicken at a time until golden brown on all sides. This usually takes about 8-15 minutes until done.

7. Remove and let drain on wire rack or paper towels.

8. Serve warm.

Note: Don't let the heating oil drop below 325°F to ensure crispy chicken and make sure to keep the flour on the crust. Fry chicken and make sure the internal temperature for chicken is 165°F. Any temperature over that will start to dry out the chickens' juices.

Chapter 5

DESSERTS

Kay's Easy Rustic Apple Tart with Caramel Sauce

Serves 4-6 // Time: 45 min minutes

Ingredients for Pie

1 ½ pk. pie crust

4 Pink Lady apples (when in season) or Granny Smith apples, peeled and thinly sliced

¼ teaspoon ground cinnamon

¼ cup sugar

3 tablespoon salted butter, cold, diced into small pieces

1 teaspoon Madagascar vanilla or pure vanilla

1 tablespoon apricot jelly, warmed (optional for glaze)

2 tablespoon rum or brandy (optional for glaze)

1 TBSP, all-purpose flour

1 egg

1 tablespoon water

Ingredients for Caramel Sauce

¾ cup unsalted butter

1 ½ cups light brown sugar

2 tablespoon water

¼ teaspoon salt

½ cup evaporated milk

1 teaspoon vanilla extract

Preparation:

1. Preheat oven to 400° F.

2. In a large bowl, add sugar, vanilla, cinnamon, and flour. Whisk to combine.

3. Combine and roll dough into a disk. Flour your work surface. Then, using a rolling pin, roll into a circle that is 8-10 inches in diameter. Turn and add more flour as necessary, so the dough doesn't stick. Transfer the dough to a parchment-lined baking sheet.

4. Slice apples thinly then put in the bowl with the sugar mixture. Toss to combine.

5. Spoon apples into the center of the crust and spread out leaving 2 inches of edges free, (If you want a more uniform look, arrange apple slices and make sure to overlap the ends).

6. Next top apples with small dice pieces of butter.

7. Fold up edges of crust over filling, leaving center uncovered.

8. In a small bowl, combine egg and with 3 tablespoons water to make an egg wash. Brush the edges with the egg wash.

9. Bake for 45 minutes to 1 hour, or until the apples are tender and the edges have browned.

(It's okay if some of the juices leak from the tart onto the baking sheet. The juices will burn on the baking sheet, but the tart is okay.)

10. For Caramel Sauce: Add butter, brown sugar, water, and salt to a medium saucepan and heat over medium-low heat, stirring until butter melts. Bring mixture to a boil, then reduce heat to a low, whisking constantly until thickened, approximately 5-7 minutes. Keep in mind that the caramel sauce will thicken more as it cools. (If the caramel sauce still looks thin after cooling, you return it to a simmer.)

11. Once sauce is removed from the heat, stir in ½ cup of evaporated milk (it will bubble a lot) and vanilla. Add in additional evaporated milk if it's too thick until desired consistency.

12. Drizzle caramel sauce over tart.

13. In a small bowl, combine apricot jelly and rum. Brush over the top of the tart as it cools. (This is an optional step.)

14. Drizzle rum mixture over the caramel sauce.

15. Serve warm with ice cream or whipped cream. Garnish with fresh mint.

Easy Lillie Cupcakes with Chocolate-Orange Cream Cheese Filling

Serves 12 // Time: 1 hour 15 minutes

Ingredients for Cupcakes

1 box vanilla cake mix

8 oz. softened cream cheese

4 oz. bittersweet chocolate, melted

2 cups powdered sugar

2 tablespoon orange juice, freshly squeezed

2 teaspoon Grand Marnier liqueur (optional)

1 teaspoon orange zest

Pinch of kosher salt

Ingredients for Chocolate Icing

¼ cup cocoa powder

2 cups powdered sugar

2 -3 tablespoon milk

Preparation:

1. Make the cupcakes according to the instructions on the package. Lightly grease the muffin tin and bake according to the package instructions. Let cool.

2. Prepare the frosting: Combine the cream cheese, orange juice, Grand Marnier liqueur, sugar, salt, and orange zest. Mix with a blender until smooth. Next, add melted chocolate and mix until blended. Refrigerate mixture for 15 minutes.

3. Scoop out the center of the cupcakes with a melon scooper. Spoon some of the icing over each cupcake, allowing the icing to set.

4. In a small mixing bowl, combine the cocoa powder, powdered sugar, and milk. Mix until smooth. Top each cupcake with icing around the edge of the cupcake to cover. Do not put the icing in the center because that will be filled with the cream cheese mixture or filling.

5. Transfer the cream cheese mixture into a pastry bag with a medium tip. Gently squeeze the cream cheese mixture onto the cupcake in a circular motion, creating a peak on the top of the cupcake. Make sure to cover the cut out. Continue with the remaining cupcakes.

6. Add additional decorate as desired.

All Grown Up Banana Pudding Cups

Serves 6 // Time: 2 hours 35 minutes

Ingredients for Banana Pudding

6 bananas, sliced

1 box mini vanilla cookies

1 tablespoon lemon juice, freshly squeezed

2 large egg yolks

1 ¾ cup milk

2 cups heavy whipping cream, very cold

3 tablespoon corn starch

¼ teaspoon kosher salt

2 teaspoon vanilla extract

1 Tablespoon Madagascar vanilla bean

¼ cup banana liqueur or 2 tablespoon banana extract

½ cup granulated sugar, plus 2 tablespoon

¼ cup powder sugar

Preparation:

For Pudding: In a medium mixing bowl, combine egg yolks, vanilla, banana extract, cornstarch, and 2 tablespoons of sugar. Set aside.

1. Heat milk, sugar, and salt in a medium saucepan. Stir and warm mixture until sugar is dissolved.

2. Temper egg mixture, whipping constantly. Add warm milk mixture to egg mixing, then transfer back into the saucepan.

3. Cook over medium-low heat, stirring constantly until the mixture reaches 172 to 180 degrees F, approximately 5 to 10 minutes. The mixture will begin to thicken and bubble around the edges.

4. Pour pudding in a medium bowl and cover with plastic wrap for 2 hours or overnight.

5. For Whipped Cream: Put the heavy whipping cream into the bowl of a stand mixer. Add the powder sugar and vanilla bean. Whisk ingredients until stiff peaks form. Cover and refrigerate until assembly.

6. Place some of the vanilla wafers on half of a sheet pan. Slowly and evenly, pour the banana liqueur over the cookies. Set aside for about 10 minutes. (Skip this step if banana extract was used.

7. In bowl toss the banana slices with the lemon juice

8. Assemble, in a single serving trifle dish Put fill ⅓ of the dish with pudding, line vanilla wafer cookies on the sides between the glass and the pudding, next layer add banana, next banana liqueur vanilla wafers, top with a layer off pudding, finish with whip cream. Repeat for the remainder of the dishes. Refrigerate for 30 minutes to overnight.

9. Garnish with 1 or 2 mini wafers before serving.

Note: This can be made as a large dish instead of single servings by using a medium glass dish. Short cut is to skip the pudding recipe and make instant French vanilla pudding and following the box instructions.

Lovely Lemon Cake with Lemon Cream Cheese Frosting

Serves 10-12 // Time: 1 hour 30 minutes

Ingredients for Cake

3 cups all-purpose flour

2 cups sugar

1 ½ teaspoon baking powder

½ teaspoon baking soda

1 teaspoon kosher salt

4 large eggs, room temperature

1 ½ sticks unsalted butter, room temperature

1 ¼ cup whole milk

¼ cup vegetable oil

1 tablespoon lemon extract

¼ cup lemon juice, freshly squeezed

Zest of one lemon

Ingredients for Frosting

1 stick of unsalted butter, softened

8 oz. cream cheese, softened

2 tablespoon lemon juice, divided

1 teaspoon vanilla extract

2 ¾ cups powdered sugar

1 Tablespoon lemon zest

Preparation:

1. For Cake: Grease three 8-inch pans. Line the bottoms with parchment paper. Preheat an oven to 350 degrees F.

2. In a large mixing bowl, use a hand mixer to cream the butter and sugar together.

3. Use a fork to combine the eggs, milk, lemon juice, vanilla extract, vegetable oil, and lemon extract together in a bowl. Set aside.

4. In another mixing bowl, stir together flour, baking powder, and salt.

5. Add ⅓ of the dry ingredients to the butter mixture and mix in until just combined. Add in half of the milk mixture and combine. Add in another ⅓

6. of the dry ingredients until combined and follow with the remainder of the milk mixture. Add in the remainder of the dry ingredients and mix with the hand mixer until just combined.

7. Using a rubber spatula, scrape the sides and the bottom of the bowl to make sure everything is mixed in. Gently fold in lemon zest.

8. Divide the batter among the three prepared pans. Bake at 350° F for 25 to 30 minutes. When finished, let cake sit in pans for 5 minutes, then transfer to a wire rack to cool completely before layering and frosting.

9. For Lemon Curd: In a medium saucepan, combine sugar, cornstarch, and water on medium heat. Stir mixture constantly for about 3-4 minutes. Mixture should thicken and come to a boil. Let boil for 1 more minute, then remove from heat.

10. In another bowl, crack the eggs and temper them by adding a few tablespoons of the hot curd mixture, stirring constantly to keep the eggs from cooking.

11. Return mixture back to the saucepan and cook on medium heat, stirring constantly for 1-2 minutes. The curd should thicken and be yellow in color. Stir in butter, lemon juice, and zest. Let cool, then cover with Saran wrap and refrigerate for 4 hours, or overnight.

12. For frosting: Using a stand mixer fitted with a paddle attachment, or a hand mixer, beat the cream cheese and butter together on medium speed until smooth and no lumps remain, or for about 3 full minutes. Reduce the mixer speed to low, then add the powdered sugar, 1 tablespoon of lemon juice, lemon zest, vanilla extract, and salt. Once the sugar begins to incorporate with the rest of the mixture, increase the mixer to a high speed and beat for 3 minutes. Add the remaining tablespoon lemon juice to thin, if desired.

13. Assemble Cake and Frost: First, using a large serrated knife, trim the tops off the cake layers to create a flat surface. Place 1 layer on your cake plate or stand. Evenly cover the top with lemon cream cheese frosting. Place the 2nd cake layer on top, place the cake the cut side down (make sure to align edges). Create a well or border along the edge of the cake using the frosting, and spoon in the lemon curd filling into the center of the well/border. (Note: don't fill taller than the border to prevent the curd from spilling out on the sides.) Next the 3rd layer, place the cuts

14. side down on top, (make sure to align the edges) and top with more frosting. Spread the frosting down around the sides.

15. Decorate as desired.

Not My Sister-in-Law's Chess Pie

Serves 8 // Time: 1 hour

Ingredients for Chess Pie

1 ½ cups sugar

1 tablespoon flour

1 tablespoon self-rise cornmeal

4 eggs, beaten

1 ½ teaspoon Madagascar bourbon vanilla bean paste or vanilla extract

12 oz. can evaporated milk

1 stick unsalted butter, melted

1 pinch kosher salt

1 9-inch unbaked pie shell

Preparation:

1. Preheat oven to 375° F. In a large bowl, combine butter and sugar. Next, add eggs to the mixture and mix well.

2. salt, and vanilla. Blend well.

3. Pour the filling into the crust and cover the edges of the crust with foil to prevent it from burning, taking care not to touch the filling.

4. Bake at 375° F for 15 minutes.

5. Reduce heat to 350° F for 45 minutes.

6. Remove the foil after 30 minutes of the total cooking time.

7. Remove from oven and let cool.

8. Serve warm or at room temperature with whipped cream.

Note: This pie can be made in advance, but it must be refrigerated. Take out 2-3 hours before serving to bring it to room temperature.

Not Your Momma's Pineapple Upside Down Cake

Servings 8-9 // Time: 1 hour

Ingredients for Cake

1 ⅓ cup all-purpose flour

½ stick unsalted butter, melted

½ stick unsalted butter, room temperature

1 ⅓ cup light brown sugar

20 oz. can pineapple slices, drain juices and reserve

¼ cup vegetable shortening (solid)

2 cups granulated sugar

2 large eggs

2 teaspoon baking powder

1 teaspoon baking soda

4 teaspoon Madagascar bourbon vanilla bean paste or vanilla extract

1 cup milk (if bourbon is not used, 1 ¼ cup milk)

¼ cup, plus 2 tablespoon bourbon (optional)

¼ cup pineapple juice, drained from pineapple slices

maraschino cherries, no stems (optional)

Preparation:

1. Preheat the oven to 350°F.

2. In a small mixing bowl, whisk together the melted butter, 2 teaspoons of the vanilla, 2 tablespoons of bourbon, and brown sugar until fully combined. Pour into a 12-inch cake pan and spread evenly. Put in the oven for 4-6 minutes until brown sugar is melted.

3. Remove from oven and do not stir. Arrange pineapple slices in pan on top of brown sugar and butter mixture. Put a cherry in the middle of each pineapple slice, set aside, and let cool.

4. In a large mixing bowl, whisk together the flour, baking powder, and salt. Set aside.

5. In a large measuring cup, combine bourbon, milk, and pineapple juice, then set aside.

6. With a stand mixer bowl, beat the butter, vegetable oil, and granulated sugar until the mixture is light and fluffy. This should take about 4-5 minutes. Add in the eggs one at a time, mixing until just combined. Mix in the rest of the vanilla. Scrape down the sides of the bowl as needed.

7. On a low- medium speed, blend in the flour mixture alternating with the milk mixture, beginning and ending with flour. Stir only enough after each addition to combine.

8. Pour the batter into the cake pan over the pineapple slices and cherries, spreading it around into one even layer.

9. Bake for 45-55 minutes, or until a wooden toothpick is inserted into the center of the cake and it comes out clean.

10. Remove the cake from the oven and wait for 3 minutes. Run a knife around the sides of the pan to make sure the cake isn't sticking. Place a serving plate over the pan and flip over. Wait about 30 seconds, then lift the pan off. The cake should slide out. If anything sticks to the pan, use a small knife to remove it out and place it back on the cake in the same place.

11. Serve warm or at room temperature. Garnish with a dollop of whipped cream and a mint sprig.

Peach Cobbler Crescents with Vanilla Ice Cream

Servings: 8 // Time: 45 minutes

Ingredients for Cobbler

2 large fresh peaches

2 8-oz. cans crescent rolls

2 sticks unsalted butter, melted

2-3 tablespoon butter

1 cup sugar

½ cup brown sugar

2 teaspoon cinnamon

2 teaspoon nutmeg

1 teaspoon vanilla extract

12 oz. can lemon-lime soda

Preparation:

Preheat the oven to 350°F.

1. Lightly butter 8 x 12-inch glass baking dish with butter. Set aside.

2. Peel and pit peaches. Slice them into wedges (8 slices per peach), then place in a medium-sized bowl.

3. Combine half of the sugar, brown sugar, cinnamon, and nutmeg in a bowl and sprinkle over the peaches. Toss the peaches to coat in seasoning and set aside.

4. Open the can of crescent rolls and unroll them. Place 1-2 peach slices onto the wide end of the crescent roll and roll it up. Place them in the baking dish.

5. Spoon the rest of the sugar mixture over each crescent.

6. Pour the lemon-lime soda into the empty spaces between the crescent rolls and along the sides of the baking dish. Be cautious not to pour soda on top of the crescents. The entire can may not be needed. If there aren't any empty spaces between the rolls, skip this step.

7. Bake for 35 to 40 minutes, or until crescents are golden brown.

8. Serve warm with vanilla ice cream topped with a sprinkle of cinnamon and sugar.

Note: For a little variation of this recipe, you can substitute the lemon-lime soda with Mountain Dew or orange soda. You may not need to use the entire can of soda. Be careful not to overpour.

Chocolate Cake

Serves 8-10 // Time: 1 hour 30 minutes

Ingredients for Cake

4 cups all-purpose flour

¾ cup unsweetened, dark chocolate cocoa powder

1 bar dark chocolate, finely chopped

3 cups sugar

1 cup dark brown sugar

2 teaspoon baking powder

1 teaspoon baking soda

1 teaspoon salt

4 large eggs

1 cup buttermilk

¼ cup vegetable oil

3 ½ sticks butter, room temperature

2 teaspoon vanilla extract

1 cup hot, freshly brewed coffee

1 cup boiling hot water

Baking oil spray

Ingredients for Chocolate Frosting

3 large bars 72% Dark Chocolate Bar, finely chopped

1 large bar 31% Milk Chocolate Bar, finely chopped

1 ¾ cups heavy cream (¼)

1 ½ cups unsalted butter, room temperature

¼ cup cocoa powder

1 teaspoon vanilla

¼ teaspoon salt

7-8 cups powdered sugar

Ingredients for Chocolate Ganache

1 cup semi-sweet chocolate chips

½ cup heavy whipping cream

Preparation:

1. Preheat oven to 350°F and prepare the 9-inch round cake pans by lining the bottoms with parchment paper, and spray with baking oil spray. Set aside.

2. For Cake: Place the finely chopped chocolate into a small microwave-safe bowl. Microwave on medium for 1 minute. Stir mixture. Continue heating in 30-second intervals until the chocolate is almost completely melted, but some small chunks may remain. Stir until smooth and set aside.

3. In a medium bowl, whisk together all-purpose flour, cocoa powder, baking soda, and salt, then set aside.

4. In a bowl, combine buttermilk, eggs, vanilla, and oil.

5. Using a stand mixer, beat butter until smooth for about 1 minute. Add sugar and dark brown sugar until smooth and fluffy, scraping sides occasionally for about 3 minutes.

6. Drizzle in the cooled, melted chocolate and continue beating on medium-high until thoroughly blended and smooth, scraping sides occasionally.

7. Add half of the flour mixture, then half of the buttermilk mixture, and repeat until all combined, scraping down the sides as needed.

8. Slowly mix in hot water and coffee until combine. Pour batter evenly into 3 baking pans. Bake for 30-35 minutes. Use a toothpick put in center of the cake. If toothpick comes out clean remove cakes from oven. Be careful not to over bake it will cause cake to be dry.

9. For the Chocolate Buttercream: In a small bowl, combine the semi-sweet chocolate with 2 tablespoons of cream, then microwave for 40 seconds on half power. Stir to combine, then set aside. Whip the butter for about 5 minutes using the paddle attachment (in a stand-up mixer).

10. Beat in the powdered sugar slowly. Add the cream. Slowly mix in the ¼ cup of cocoa powder. Add salt and vanilla. Mix until you have a fluffy, even consistency, then beat in melted chocolate.

11. For Ganache: Add the chocolate chips to a medium-sized bowl and set aside. Put the heavy whipping cream to a microwave safe bowl or measuring cup and heat for about 1 minute. Pour the warm cream over the chocolate chips and allow to sit for 3-5 minutes. Gently stir the cream and chocolate together until they come together to a smooth consistency. Try not to whisk too vigorously, which can add air bubbles to the ganache. Let set for 10 minutes.

12. Frost the cake: First, using a large serrated knife, trim the tops off the cake layers to create a flat surface. Place the first layer of cake onto your cake plate or stand. Evenly cover the top of the cake with chocolate frosting. Place the second cake layer on top, cut the sides down, and repeat for the third layer. Top with more frosting and spread the frosting down around the sides.

13. Drizzle the chocolate ganache around the edges of the cake, then pour the remainder of the ganache on top of the cake and spread evenly.

14. Decorate as desired.

How to Prep Collard Greens

1. Check both sides of the leaf to make sure greens are tough. You will have to cut stems off of some of the greens. For the large and mature leaves, take each leaf and fold lengthwise at the stem. Tear the tough portion of the stem away from the leaf and discharge. If you like you can, cut the stem away with a knife.

2. Stack several leaves on top of each other and roll together into spiral. Cut into one-inch pieces, cross-cutting, then turn the cut spirals and cut at right angles.

How to Wash Collard Greens

1. Put cut greens into a clean sink and cover with cold water. I like to add half a cup of vinegar, ¼ cup to ½ cup of baking soda, and 4 tablespoons of kosher salt to the water. (The vinegar and baking soda don't change the flavor of the greens, and it works like a charm on cleaning) Scrub the greens (by using the old school method of hand washing clothes) to loosen up any dirt or rocks that may be in the greens.

2. Drain the water and fill again with fresh cold water to rinse the greens. Repeat steps 3 and4 two more times to ensure that the greens are clean. Nothing should be on them, but plain water. Add them to the recipe!

Kay's Kitchen Conversion Charts

Kay's Meaurement

teaspoon	t
tablespoon	T
cup	c
pound	lbs

Volumes

A Pinch	1/16 TSP
A Dash	1/8 TSP
1 TSP	5 ML
1 TBS	15 ML
1 CUP	240 ML

Temperature

Fahrenheit	Celsius
100 °F	38 °C
150 °F	66 °C
200 °F	93 °C
250 °F	121 °C
300 °F	149 °C
325 °F	163 °C
350 °F	177 °C
375 °F	191 °C
400 °F	204 °C
425 °F	218 °C
450 °F	232 °C
475 °F	246 °C
500 °F	260 °C
525 °F	274 °C
550 °F	288 °C

Measurement

Cup	Ounces	Milliliters	Tablespoons	Teaspoons
1/16 cup	1/2 oz	15 ml	1	3
1/8 cup	1 oz	30 ml	3	6
1/4 cup	2 oz	59 ml	4	12
1/3 cup	2.5 oz	79 ml	5.5	16
3/8 cup	3 oz	90 ml	6	18
1/2 cup	4 oz	118 ml	8	24
2/3 cup	5 oz	158 ml	11	32
3/4 cup	6 oz	177 ml	12	36
1 cups	8 oz	240 ml	16	48
2 cups	16 oz	480 ml	32	96
4 cups	32 oz	960 ml	64	192
5 cups	40 oz	1180 ml	80	236
6 cups	48 oz	1420 ml	96	284
8 cups	64 oz	1895 ml	128	379

Volume By Weight

1 LBS =	454 GRAMS	=	3 1/2 CUPS FLOUR	=	2 1/2 CUPS SUGAR

1 Cup:
8 Ounces
240 ml
16 TBS
48 TSP

1/4 Cup:
2 Ounces
60 ml
4 TBS
12 TSP

1 Gallon:
4 Quarts
8 Pints
16 Cups
128 Ounces
3.8 Litres

1 Quart:
2 Pints
4 Cups
32 Ounces
.95 Litres

1 Pint:
2 Cups
16 Ounces
480 ml

1 TBS:
0.5 Oz
15 ml
3 TSP

What's Kay Cook'N Vol. 1 Index

THANK YOU FOR PURCHASING MY COOKBOOK

If you are here, then you have taken a great step. You have purchased my cookbook. You can expand your knowledge and tastes just by using my cookbook. With the cookbook, you hold the research and knowledge shared amongst many food lovers and good old fashion home cooks.

There is a whole world of untapped and unexplored cooking methods, tips, and recipes that this cookbook and my future cookbooks will introduce you to.

Taking advantage of the cookbook to become better at cooking and finding more taste is a huge deal that you won't regret. I am filled with joy and truly grateful that you have purchased my cookbook and I hope you enjoy using it as much as I enjoy sharing it with you. Thank you.

Please follow me on all social media sites "What's Kay CookN" and don't forget to watch my videos on YouTube.

WHATS KAY COOK'N

CPSIA information can be obtained
at www.ICGtesting.com
Printed in the USA
LVRC062048300321
682993LV00005B/17